the
parenting
teenagers
course

for those parenting
11 to 18-year-olds

> Leaders' Guide

Published in North America by Alpha North America, 2275 Half Day Road, Suite 185, Deerfield, IL 60015

© 2011 Alpha International, Holy Trinity Brompton, Brompton Road, London, SW7 1JA, UK

The Parenting Teenagers Course Leaders' Guide

First printed by Alpha North America in 2011

Printed in the United States of America

Scripture in this publication is from the Holy Bible, New International Version (NIV), Copyright 1973, 1978, 1984, 2011 Biblica, Inc., used by permission of Zondervan. All rights reserved.

ISBN 978-1-933114-42-2

1 2 3 4 5 6 7 8 9 10 Printing/Year 15 14 13 12 11

Contents

Welcome

We're so glad that you've decided to run The Parenting Teenagers Course and we hope you enjoy the experience as much as we do. Parents feel under more pressure than ever today and many are in need of help and support. Seeing them grow in confidence and feel less isolated through doing the course has made us want to keep going and to make this resource available to others to run in their home, community, or church.

This Leaders' Guide is designed to help you to run a successful course. It is important that those who lead the discussions are familiar with the key ingredients of the course and the role of the small group hosts. It is also useful as a quick reference. We find it helpful to have it with us when we are running a session as the checklists and timetables help keep us on track.

If you start to run a course, please register it online at **alphausa.org/relationshipcentral (in Canada–relationshipcentral.ca)**. This enables potential guests who live in your area to find a course nearby. It also enables us to let you know of ways in which we can support you.

Please do contact us if you have any questions and do let us know how you get along. We love to hear feedback from other courses.

Nicky and Sila Lee
Creators of The Parenting Teenagers Course

Introduction

The Parenting Teenagers Course, designed for those parenting eleven to eighteen-year-olds, was started at HTB, London, in 1997 and the material was first published in 2011. We have had many requests from people all around the world wanting to use this resource as well as The Parenting Children Course, designed for those parenting children up to ten years old.

The Parenting Teenagers Course is for any parent or guardian of children aged eleven to eighteen, whether they consider themselves to have strong parenting skills or are struggling, and whether they are parenting as a couple, as a single parent, or as a step-parent. Guests can come alone or as a couple. The practical tools of the course are applicable to everyone who has responsibility for a child in this age group.

The course is made up of five weekly sessions lasting two-and-a-half hours, including the meal. However, each session can be split into two and run over ten shorter sessions lasting one-and-a-half hours.

Each session ideally starts with something to eat and drink, as this gives guests a chance to relax and talk to other parents in a friendly, welcoming setting. Creating a great atmosphere is an important part of the course. Equally important is the reassurance for guests that nobody will have to disclose any information about their home life/parenting that they do not wish to. Many people, however, have discovered that discussing their experiences with fellow parents in a small group is one of the great benefits of the course.

After the meal, the leaders welcome the guests, give any announcements and then provide an opportunity for a quick review of the previous session(s). They then show the relevant section of the DVD or give the talk themselves.

During each session there are breaks in the talks to give the guests an opportunity to discuss the issues that have been raised. For courses with more than ten guests, it is best to divide into two or more smaller groups. The groups are organized according to the age of the guests' oldest child. Each small group needs a host who acts as a facilitator for the discussion.

How to run the course

The course is designed so that it is easy to run, particularly when using the DVDs. You may decide to do your own talks eventually, but we would recommend starting with the DVDs as this means you can concentrate on hosting your guests and creating the right atmosphere.

Whichever way you decide to run the course, you will need to provide a guest manual for each person. These contain the questions for the group discussions and the exercises that the guests fill in during and after each session.

Using the DVDs

All the sessions of the course are available on DVD. Nicky and Sila's talks were filmed in a TV studio and each session includes street interviews and filmed clips of parenting experts as well as "sofa" families, which comprise parents and children, aged eleven to eighteen, talking about their experiences of parenting and being parented.

The DVDs indicate when to pause for an exercise break or discussion. You can see the timetables of these listed in the timetable for each session on pages 22–41 of this guide.

Giving live talks

If you are giving live talks, they should ideally be presented by a mother and a father. To prepare:

- watch the DVD of the particular session. You may also want to read the relevant section of *The Parenting Book*
- decide who will do each section of the talk, ensuring that you both have a turn to speak, as it is helpful to have the perspective of a father and a mother on the different topics. You will

generally not be able to swap back and forth between you as frequently as on the DVD
- agree on what stories you are going to share from your own family. Be sure these would not embarrass your children now or in the future. Tell stories against yourself, not against your children, or the other parent
- it is possible to play in some of the filmed clips of parenting experts and the "sofa" parents and children by using the "Filmed Clip Inserts" on the DVD
- decide which clips to play. There will not be time to use them all

Structure of a typical session

Five-week courses

The whole session, including the meal, lasts approximately two-and-a-half hours. We strongly suggest that you do not shorten the length of the discussions as these are often the most beneficial aspect of the course. Pages 22–31 show suggested timetables for five-week courses.

Ten-week courses

Each of the five sessions is divided into two roughly equal parts, allowing the course to be run over ten weeks with each session lasting approximately one-and-a-half hours. Pages 32–41 show suggested timetables for ten-week courses.

1. Welcome

Some guests are apprehensive when they first arrive, so a drink and a warm welcome will help them to feel relaxed.

Helpful tip:
Men in particular can be hesitant about coming on the course so having other men to welcome them can make a big difference.

2. The meal

Evening courses

The meal is an important time for guests to get to know other parents and to be put at ease. It is crucial to create a warm, friendly atmosphere. It is generally best to serve a main course and then to serve cake, cookies, or brownies with coffee and tea half way through the evening during the fifteen-minute exercise/discussion.

Morning courses

The meal could be breakfast or a snack and consist of tea and coffee, pastries, fruit and yogurt, muesli, muffins, coffeecake and cookies, etc. As with courses run in the evening, the meal provides an opportunity for guests to relax and meet other parents/guardians of children aged eleven to eighteen.

3. Announcements and review

From Week 2 onwards guests are given a few minutes to review the previous session(s). *The Parenting Teenagers Course Guest Manual* contains a summary of what has already been covered. The guests can share their thoughts and experiences in twos or threes, or as a small group.

4. Talk (Part 1) and short exercises/discussions

Five-week courses

The talk for each session is divided into two parts. Each part is approximately thirty minutes and the DVDs indicate clearly when to pause between the parts. Following Part 1 there is a fifteen-minute break when the guests are served tea or coffee and something to eat, such as brownies, cake, or cookies. Sometimes there is an exercise in the manual to complete and then to discuss, either as a small group or in twos or threes. (Discussing in twos or threes allows couples who are parenting together to discuss an issue with each other, while those parenting on their own can discuss with one or two others.)

Ten-week courses

Either Part 1 or Part 2 is played, depending on which week it is. When using Part 1, the short exercise/discussion is extended from fifteen minutes to at least half an hour to allow for a group discussion. The manual has questions marked "For ten-week courses only."

5. Talk (Part 2)

Five-week courses

The session continues with Part 2 of the talk. If the guests are midway through discussing a topic that is important to one or more of them, the small group hosts can pick this up again in the longer discussion at the end of the evening. This works better than delaying Part 2 and having to shorten the last discussion. Sometimes the talk in Part 2 will help the discussion.

6. Group discussion

Five- and ten-week courses

These take place for half an hour or so at the end of each session. Small groups are led by small group hosts, who facilitate the discussion using the "Small group discussion" questions in the guest manual as a guide. The aim is not to have all the answers, rather to give every guest who wants to the opportunity to speak. The hosts may occasionally share from their own experiences when appropriate. Arranging the small groups according to the age of the guests' oldest child ensures that each small group is at a similar stage of parenting and parents have similar issues to discuss. If the small group host is a parent, he or she should ideally have a child at least as old as the children of the guests in their group.

7. Ending

Five- and ten-week courses

It is important to bring the session to an end by the time stated so that the guests feel comfortable leaving promptly. This is best done by the leader stating what the time is and standing up, however animated or inconclusive the discussion may be at that point. Some parents will need to leave promptly because of childcare arrangements.

Those who are not in a hurry may want to continue discussing an issue informally. Many of the issues raised during the small group discussion will not have a neat solution. Raising the issue and hearing the experiences of other parents can help guests to know that they are not alone in the challenges they are facing and to gain a longer perspective.

8. Homework

There are homework exercises in the guest manual for guests to complete between the sessions. These are an important part of the course as they help guests to apply the topics raised on the session to their own situation. (When encouraging guests to complete the homework, assure them it is not the sort that is collected and graded!)

9. Feedback

Five- and ten-week courses

A questionnaire is available for distribution during the final session. This serves as a review of the course for the guests and provides helpful feedback for the leaders. Guests are asked to fill most of it in during the meal and then complete it at the end of the session. The appropriate questionnaire can be downloaded from our website: **alphausa.org/relationshipcentral)in Canada relationshipcentral.ca**).

Creating the right atmosphere

A warm and welcoming environment is very important to the success of the course. It is essential that guests feel relaxed and are able to talk freely about sensitive issues. The right atmosphere helps to make this possible.

1. Choose the best venue

The key is to find a location that allows you to create a welcoming atmosphere and serve a meal:

- if you are running a small course, a home is usually the best location
- larger courses can be held in a church hall, restaurant, coffee shop after hours, school, hotel, etc.

2. Think friendly, fun, and relaxed

- if the course is not held in a home and the space is unappealing, find someone who enjoys the challenge of transforming it to look welcoming, friendly, and relaxed. Even the most uninspiring room can be turned into a great venue with a little creativity
- chairs arranged in a circle for the small groups, ideally around a low coffee-style table, give each guest a sense of belonging (this is particularly helpful if they have come on their own) and make it easier to facilitate the small group discussions. This arrangement also helps guests to chat and build friendships more easily, both over the meal and during the discussions. They can turn their chairs if necessary for the talks. (See page 42 for a suggested room set-up)
- low lighting and background music during the meal and at the end help to create a relaxed atmosphere

3. Provide food
- serving food before the course gives guests the opportunity to unwind and get to know others
- on evening courses it also means people can come straight from work without having to worry about eating before the course. We recommend serving the main course at the start of each session.Coffee, tea, and a simple dessert, cake or cookies can then be served during the short exercise/discussion midway through the evening

4. Give great service
- some guests worry about coming to The Parenting Teenagers Course. Having a friendly team who go out of their way to make the guests feel welcome helps to put them at ease
- on the five-week courses, serve the guests coffee and tea during the short break. This is a sign to the guests that you care about them and that their family life is important to you.

Helpful Tip:
Cover the low coffee-style table with a table cloth, napkins, a flower, and a candle as this adds a special touch and helps create a great atmosphere, like a restaurant.

Hosting the small groups

Small group hosts play a vital role in the guests' experience of the course. For courses that have more than one small group, it will be important to get the hosts together prior to the course to ensure that they understand their role in welcoming and hosting the guests throughout each session as well as facilitating the discussions. Each small group host should have a copy of this Leaders' Guide.

Ideally there should be two or more hosts per group, including at least one man and one woman if the group is made up of fathers and mothers.

1. The role of the hosts

- the main role of the small group hosts is to welcome and host the guests in their group, to introduce them to each other, to serve them tea or coffee, to find out how their week has been, and to facilitate the small group discussion during the last part of each session
- on the first session, during the first discussion, the small group host should encourage people to contribute only what they feel comfortable sharing with others. Ask the guests to respect the other members by keeping any personal information that is disclosed in the group confidential
- the small group hosts are not instructors. Their job is to get the conversation flowing and encourage discussion, not to teach the guests about parenting (the talks aim to do that!). Small group hosts are welcome to suggest ideas from their own experiences of parenting/caring for children, but they need to ensure that it is in line with the course material. Their aim is to be encouraging and affirming, so the most helpful way of sharing their own stories and tips is to use "I" or "We" statements (such as, "I/We have found this helpful . . .") rather than instructional statements ('You need to stop doing that and do this instead"). Using "I" statements leaves the guests free to agree or disagree with what the host has suggested, rather than feeling that they are being judged

2. Preparation

- the small group hosts should familiarize themselves with the questions in the guest manual ahead of each session
- they will also find it helpful to read *The Parenting Book* in advance of the course so that they are familiar with the topics the course covers. There is more material in the book than the course is able to cover. The book covers parenting children from birth to eighteen years, so it puts the teenage years in a longer perspective

3. Practical details

- arrange the chairs so that guests can see and hear each other
- ensure the host(s) can see everyone
- provide adequate lighting so that guests can read the manual and write ideas down if they wish

- check ventilation so that the room is neither stuffy nor too cold
- stay on time – aim to start and end the discussion on time
- if the group has more than ten guests and there are enough hosts, it may be better to split it in half so that more people get a chance to contribute

4. Groups can be ruined by two types of leadership
- weak leadership – not properly prepared, allows one person to do all the talking
- dominant leadership – does all the talking instead of giving others the opportunity to say what is on their mind

5. Ask open questions
- "open questions" require more than a "yes" or "no" answer and allow for a variety of responses, e.g., "What's the greatest challenge you're facing right now as a parent?" "What's the main reason you attended the course?" "What do you hope to get out of the course?"
- use the questions in the guest manual to get the discussion going unless one of the guests has already raised an issue that is of interest to most of the group
- do not feel you have to get through all the "Small group discussion" questions in the guest manual. Use as many as you need to keep the discussion moving, drawing in as many of the group as possible
- if running short of time and the discussion has been around only one or two of the questions for discussion, leave a few minutes at the end to ask, "Did anyone want to discuss one of the other questions in the manual?" If so, tell the group you will come back to that question on the following session (either during the meal or as part of the small group discussion)
- have ready some follow-up questions of your own in case the discussion dries up
- two basic questions are: "What do you think?" and "What do you feel about what you have just heard?"
- rather than answering a question from a guest, direct it back to the group by asking: "What does everyone else think?"
- avoid being patronizing. Treat everyone with respect and interest even though you may disagree with their views

6. Be prepared for questions

- if an issue is raised that is beyond your experience or knowledge, don't be afraid to say so. If necessary, tell the guest(s) you will investigate sources of information about the issue before the next session
- see if the issue is covered by *The Parenting Book* or try another of the books listed in the back of the guest manual. (There is further recommended reading on our website: **alphausa.org/relationshipcentral (in Canada– relationshipcentral.ca**).
- come back to the issue the following week either by talking to the individual guest over the meal or by raising it again in the small group discussion
- if the issue requires professional help, encourage the guest to talk to a doctor or a trained counselor

Making referrals

Prior to the course, leaders should discover any other local sources of help for issues that are beyond their experience and beyond the scope of the course.

Guests may wish to discuss with a trained counselor an issue that has been raised by the course, or another issue they are facing. For some parents, coming on The Parenting Teenagers Course will be the first step in seeking help for their situation.

If possible, have the contact details of a counselor who deals with parenting issues, an educational psychologist, or a parenting coach. You may be able to find a counselor in the U.S. through your church. Their child's school may have an educational psychologist to whom they can be referred. Otherwise recommend guests consult their doctor, particularly if the issue relates to their own or their child's physical or emotional health.

Promoting the course

To help advertise your course:
- get your church leader on board. Help the leadership of your church to catch the vision of the course and to see the benefits that it can bring to members of your church and to other parents in your area
- ask to have the course advertised from the front during Sunday services. Promote the course dates in every way you can through the church website and newsletter, on bulletin boards and through displaying invitations prominently
- use the promotional film clip to excite parents and other care givers of children. This three-minute clip gives people a taste of what is covered on the course and creates an interest to find out more
- think of places that might be interested in displaying posters and course invitations:
    - *local churches*
    - *schools*
    - *doctors' offices*
    - *the local library*
    - *charity shops*
- try to get an article about the course in your local newspaper or an interview with your local radio station
- ask to display course invitations and posters in other places where parents are likely to go, such as:
    - *news stands*
    - *fitness centers*
    - *other local shops*
    - *the local recreation center/swimming pool*
- don't forget that the main reason people come to the course is through a personal recommendation. Make sure that during the last session everybody on the current course is offered invitations to the next course to give away. Encourage them to tell at least one other parent. In this way your course will grow organically
- Register your course on **alphausa.org/relationshipcentral (in Canada—relationshipcentral.ca)** so that people who are looking for a local course online find yours

Quick checklist

As well as the timetable in this Leaders' Guide you will need the following:

☐ *The Parenting Teenagers Course DVD* set

☐ *The Parenting Teenagers Course Guest Manuals* (one per person)

☐ Music (and a way to play it) – to be used during the meal and at the end of each session. A playlist on an MP3 player is the easiest option

☐ Food and drinks (cold and hot, including coffee and tea)
Evening courses – main course and brownies, cake, or cookies
Morning courses – breakfast or a mid-morning snack
e.g.: pastries, fruit and yogurt, coffee cake, and cookies

☐ Tables and chairs, suitable lighting, tablecloths, napkins, candles, flowers and vases

☐ Plates, glasses, cups, and flatware

☐ Attendance list and name labels. Wearing name labels helps people to get to know each other. For larger courses, having the small group hosts' names (or Group 1, 2, 3 etc.) written underneath the guests' names helps them to find the right group

☐ Pens

☐ Spare guest manuals for guests who forget to bring theirs back, with a blank piece of paper slipped in for guests to write their own notes (without marking the manual)

☐ Table to display some of the recommended books (optional)

☐ Spare DVD(s) of the course for guests who may have missed a session. These can be loaned with a deposit so you can replace any that are not returned

☐ DVD player

☐ TV, or screen and projector

☐ Speakers' lectern and microphone (for larger courses only)

Overview and timetable for five-week courses

(two-and-a-half-hour sessions)

Session 1 – Keeping the End in Mind

1. Overview

Session 1 helps parents to recognize their long-term aim and the value of maintaining and building their relationship with their teenager(s). Part 1 looks at the changes that adolescence brings, the pressures on teenagers and parents today and how parents can help their teenager(s) grow into mature, responsible adults. Part 2 addresses the importance of our home being a place of safety and acceptance, the place where teenagers learn about good values, a place of fun, and a place where teenagers learn about how to build healthy relationships.

2. Checklist

- materials from Quick checklist on pages 20–21

3. Timetable

(The timetable that follows is for courses being run in the evening. The starting time may of course be adjusted)

6:30   Leaders and hosts meet to pray together

6:45   Be ready! (Guests often arrive early for the first session.)
Offer guests a drink

7:00   Meal (in their small groups, if there are more than ten guests on the course)

7:30   Welcome and announcements

– *"Welcome to The Parenting Teenagers Course. Each session will be a combination of talks and discussing parenting issues with other parents. But, relax! Be assured you will not be required to disclose anything private about your children or family life"*

- *"Let us know if you can't come for one of the sessions and we will loan you the DVD"* (if available)

- *"If you have a concern about your parenting that is not covered by the course, we have the details of a local family counselor we could put you in touch with"*

- *"We'll spend the next few minutes going around the group and asking you to introduce yourself and the names and ages of your child or children. Then please say the main challenge you are facing as a parent/care giver of children aged eleven to eighteen. As people will be sharing personal information about their family life, we ask that you would respect what others say by keeping it confidential within the group"*

Note: The timings follow the exact length of the talks on the DVDs.

7:45   Start the DVD (or your live talk) – *Part 1: Understanding the transition* (27 minutes)

8:12   Exercise and discussion

"Please complete the exercise in your manual, Building Character, *and then discuss what you have written, in groups of two or three. If you are here as a couple, we suggest you discuss with your partner what you have put and talk about any changes you would like to make"*

(Small group hosts serve tea, coffee, and dessert)

8:27   Talk – *Part 2: Building strong relationships* (32 minutes)

8:59   Discussion in small groups (see questions in the guest manual)

9:30   End punctually. Encourage guests to complete the Homework Exercises 1 and 2 in the guest manual before the next session. Remind them to bring their manuals back for the next session

Live talks: Finish session with a short prayer if appropriate. For example:
"Lord, we thank You that our children are a gift from You; thank You that they are each unique and have their own unique personality and gifts. Thank You for the privilege of parenting them, of shaping and influencing their lives. We ask You to help us with this challenging task. And we pray

that, as a result of this course, each parent would feel more
confident and better equipped for this role. We ask this in
Jesus' name, Amen"

Session 2 – Meeting our Teenagers' Needs

1. Overview

Teenagers need the confidence that comes from knowing they are loved. Their behavior often acts like the gauge showing how full of love their internal "emotional tank" is. Part 1 explains the concept of the five love languages as a way of expressing love to our teenagers in order for them to feel loved. Parents are encouraged to work out which particular expression of love makes the most difference to their teenager(s), as well as recognizing which one they find the most difficult to give to their teenager(s). Part 2 looks at the different ways adults and teenagers tend to communicate and how important it is for parents to listen well and show empathy for their teenagers' feelings.

2. Checklist

- materials from Quick checklist on pages 20–21

3. Timetable

6:30 Leaders and hosts meet to pray together

6:45 Offer a drink to guests who arrive early

7:00 Meal in groups

7:30 Announcements and review

– *"Welcome back if you were here for the first session.*
A special welcome if you're here for the first time"

– *"There are spare manuals for you to borrow if you forgot to*
bring yours. Please write any notes on the blank sheet and
then you can transfer these into your own manual later on"

– *"We will start each session with a review of the previous*
session or sessions. Please look in your manual at the
summary of what we covered last week. Talk in your group
about what was most relevant for you and if you have
organized any 'Family Time' over this past week. If you did,
how did it go?"

7:40 Start the DVD (or your live talk) – *Part 1: The five love languages* (33 minutes)

8:13 Exercise and discussion

"Please complete the exercise in your manual, Ranking the Love Languages, *and then discuss what you have written in groups of two or three. If you are here as a couple, we suggest you discuss with your partner what you have written and talk about any differences you think it would make to your child or children"*

(Small group hosts serve tea, coffee, and dessert)

8:28 Talk – *Part 2: Effective communication* (26 minutes)

8:54 *"Please complete the exercise in your manual,* Reflecting Back. *In pairs one person pretends to be a teenager and the other person pretends to be the parent. The 'teenager' takes no more than a minute to tell the 'parent' something he or she is upset or worried about. The parent listens and then reflects back what they think the teenager is feeling. Resist the desire to give advice or to reassure. The aim is to practice empathizing with what the teenager is feeling but may or may not be able to articulate. After continuing the conversation for a minute or two, swap roles."*

9:05 Discussion in small groups (see questions in the guest manual)

9:30 End punctually. Encourage guests to complete the Homework Exercises 1 and 2 in their guest manual before the next session

Live talks: Finish session with a short prayer if appropriate. For example:
"Lord, we thank You that You are always listening to us and that we can pour out our hearts to You. Thank You for all the ways You assure us of Your love. We pray that You would help us to love our children with our time, words, touch, presents, and actions, and that You'd give us insight to know which love language is most significant for each child to feel loved. And in those families where communication between a parent and a teenager has broken down, we pray for a breakthrough and for a new start. We ask this in Jesus' name, Amen"

Session 3 – Setting Boundaries

1. Overview

This session looks at how parenting teenagers involves gradually letting out the boundaries and giving them increasing freedom and responsibility. Part 1 compares different parenting styles (neglectful, authoritarian, indulgent, and authoritative) and shows how a combination of warmth and firmness (authoritative parenting) is the most beneficial for a teenager's healthy development. Parents are encouraged to see themselves on the same side as their teenagers, helping them on their journey to maturity by allowing them to make their own decisions in as many areas as are safe for them to do so. Part 2 addresses how the parents' role gradually changes from "controller" to "consultant," the importance of negotiation with teenagers, and the need to have appropriate consequences when a boundary has been crossed.

2. Checklist

- materials from Quick checklist on pages 20–21

3. Timetable

6:30 Leaders and hosts meet to pray together

6:45 Offer a drink to guests who arrive early

7:00 Meal in groups

7:30 Announcements and review

- *"In the last session we looked at how we make our children feel loved. We recommend* The Five Love Languages of Teenagers *by Gary Chapman for a greater understanding of how to show love effectively to each child"*

- *"Please look in your manual at the summary of what we covered last week. Discuss in your group if you have tried using one of the five love languages in a new way since then. If so, what was the effect?"*

7:45 Start the DVD (or your live talk) – *Part 1: Letting go gradually* (30 minutes)

8:15 Exercise and discussion

"Please complete the exercise in your manual, Exercising authority, *and then discuss what you've written, in groups of two or three. If you're here as a couple, we suggest you discuss together what you've written. If you're here on your own, please discuss with one or two others"*

(Small group leaders serve tea, coffee, and dessert)

8:30 Talk – *Part 2: Encouraging responsibility*
(27 minutes)

8:57 Discussion in small groups (see questions in the guest manual)

9:30 End punctually. Encourage guests to complete the Homework Exercises 1 and 2 in the guest manual before the next session

Live talks: Finish session with a short prayer if appropriate. For example:

"Lord, we thank You that You guide us and show us the best way to live. Thank You that You give us Your love and Your boundaries that we might live life to the full. Please help us to guide our teenagers so that they grow in trust and responsibility and become people who look out for others. Help us to give You our fears and our longings so that, as we let our children go, they may know a sense of freedom in becoming the people You've made them to be. We ask this in Jesus' name. Amen"

Session 4 – Developing Emotional Health

1. Overview

Emotional health includes learning how to handle anger. Part 1 addresses inappropriate responses to anger—"rhino" behavior and "hedgehog" behavior—and how parents must learn to manage their own anger as well as helping their teenagers to learn to handle theirs. Part 2 looks at six principles for resolving conflict effectively, which can be modeled between adults and used with teenagers. The final section is on helping teenagers manage stress through allowing them to accept failure, not comparing them with others, creating enough space for relaxation, and talking to them about their worries.

2. Checklist

- materials from Quick checklist on pages 20–21

3. Timetable

6:30   Leaders and hosts meet to pray together

6:45   Offer a drink to guests who arrive early

7:00   Meal in groups

7:30   Announcements and review

- *"Next week we will have some of the recommended books on sale. You can pay by cash/check/credit card"* (as applicable)

- *"Please look in your manual at the summary of what we covered last week. Then try to think of an example of a boundary you needed to impose since then, and discuss in your group what the result was"*

7:45   Start the DVD (or your live talk) – *Part 1: Handling anger (ours and theirs)* (29 minutes)

8:14   Exercise and discussion.

"Please complete the exercise in your manual, Expressions of Anger, and then discuss what you've written in groups of two or three. If you're here as a couple, we suggest you discuss together what you've written. If you're here on your own, please discuss with one or two others"

(Small group hosts serve tea, coffee, and dessert)

8:29   Talk – *Part 2: Resolving conflict and handling stress*
       (31 minutes)

9:00   Discussion in small groups (see questions in the guest manual)

9:30   End punctually. Encourage guests to complete Homework
       Exercises 1 to 3 in the guest manual before the next session

       Live talks: Finish session with a short prayer if appropriate.
       For example:
       *"Lord, we thank You that You are the God of love and the
       Prince of peace. Thank You that You show us the way to
       resolve conflict and to build strong relationships in our
       family. We pray that You would help us to grow in our
       relationships with our children. May we learn to handle
       our anger and our stress in a healthy way, and equip our
       teenagers to do the same. And where a relationship between
       a parent and a teenager has become strained, please bring
       Your encouragement and hope for the future. Draw them
       closer again we pray. We ask this in Jesus' name, Amen"*

Session 5 – Helping Them Make Good Choices

1. Overview

The final session focuses on the choices teenagers will have to make, particularly concerning the big issues today of drugs, alcohol, sex, and the use of the Internet. Part 1 looks at the influence parents have and how they need to pass on information and values in order to protect their teenagers and give them a longer perspective. Part 2 addresses a number of ways parents can be effective in equipping their teenagers to make good choices in the long term, including talking them through situations, finding good role models, creating healthy family traditions, and praying for them regularly.

2. Checklist

- materials from Quick checklist on pages 20–21

3. Timetable

6:30   Leaders and hosts meet to pray together

6:45   Offer a drink to guests who arrive early

7:00   Meal in groups

7:30   Announcements (as applicable) and review

- *"Do please take advantage of the opportunity to buy some of the recommended books at the end of the session"*

- *"Please take as many invitations for the next Parenting Teenagers Course as you like to give to anyone who you think would be interested in coming"*

- *"The Marriage Course is a very good follow-up to this course for anybody parenting as a couple. If that applies to you, please come on our next course and take more invitations to give to others"*

- *"The Alpha course provides an opportunity to explore the meaning of life and to discuss the claims of the Christian faith. Doing Alpha has helped many parents to work out what beliefs and values they want to pass on to their children. Please take an invitation to our next course"*

– "It would be helpful if you could take a few minutes to complete the feedback questionnaire. This acts as a review for you of the whole course and your comments will help us to run the course more effectively in the future. We will give you a few minutes to fill in your comments on this session before we finish"

A copy of the questionnaire can be downloaded from our website: **alphausa.org/relationshipcentral (in Canada– relationshipcentral.ca)**

7:45 Start the DVD (or your live talk) – *Part 1: Giving a longer perspective* (35 minutes)

8:20 Exercise and discussion

"Please complete the exercise in your manual, Longer-term Values, *and then discuss what you've written in groups of two or three. If you're here as a couple, we suggest you discuss together what you've written. If you're here on your own, please discuss with one or two others"*

(Small group hosts serve tea, coffee, and dessert)

8:35 Talk – *Part 2: Equipping our children* (22 minutes)

8:57 Discussion in small groups (see questions in the guest manual)

9:30 End punctually. Ask the guests to complete the questionnaire and hand it in before they leave.

Live talks: Finish session with a short prayer if appropriate. For example:
"Lord, we thank You that love always protects, always trusts, always hopes, always perseveres, that love never fails. Thank You that You know and understand the challenges faced by each parent as they guide their teenagers to make good choices. We pray that You would help each of us to keep loving our children when things are difficult so that we might build, or rebuild, a close connection now and in the future. Lord, please fulfill Your purposes for each child and may their characters grow to reflect Your love and kindness. We ask this in Jesus' name, Amen"

Overview and timetable for
ten-week courses

(one-and-a-half-hour sessions)

Some course leaders prefer to run the course over ten weeks rather than five. This might be the case if you are running it in the morning. The five sessions are split into Part 1 and Part 2 and one part only is used each week.

(The timetable that follows is for courses being run in the morning.)

Note: The times follow the exact length of the talks on the DVDs

Week 1
Session 1 – Keeping the End in Mind, Part 1

10:00 Welcome guests and offer them something to eat and drink (e.g., coffee, tea, pastries, fruit and yogurt, muesli, muffins)

10:15 Welcome and announcements

- *"Welcome to The Parenting Teenagers Course. Each session will be a combination of talks and discussing parenting issues with other parents. But, relax! Be assured you will not be required to disclose anything private about your children or family life"*

- *"Let us know if you can't come for one of the mornings and we will loan you the DVD" (if available)*

- *"If you have a concern about your parenting that is not covered by the course, we have the details of a local family counselor we could put you in touch with"*

- *"We'll spend the next few minutes going around the group(s) asking you to introduce yourself and the names and ages of your child or children. Then please say the main challenge you are facing as a parent/care giver of children aged eleven to eighteen"*

10:25　Start the DVD (or your live talk) – *Session 1 Part 1: Understanding the transition* (27 minutes)

10:52　Exercise and discussion

Ask guests to complete the exercise *Building Character* and then have a small group discussion (see questions for ten-week courses in the guest manual)

11:30　End punctually. Encourage guests to complete Exercise 1 of the homework before next time.

If appropriate, finish with a short prayer.
(There is no prayer at the end of Part 1 on the DVD.)
For example:
"Lord, we thank You for every teenager and every pre-teen represented by those doing this course. Thank You that each one is unique and special. We pray that You would help us to build our relationship with them through all the ups and downs of adolescence, and that we would see their characters developing. We pray that they would grow into mature, responsible adults. We ask this in Jesus' name, Amen"

Week 2
Session 1 – Keeping the End in Mind, Part 2

10:00　Welcome guests and offer something to eat and drink

10:15　Announcements and review

- *"Welcome back if you were here for the first session. A special welcome if you are here for the first time"*

- *"There are spare manuals for you to borrow if you forgot to bring yours. Please write any notes on the blank sheet and then you can transfer these into your own manual later on"*

- *"We will start each session with a quick review of the previous session or sessions. Please look back in your manual to remind yourself what we covered on Week 1. Then discuss (as a group, or with one or two others) whether you have made any changes in your parenting since last week"*

10:25   Start the DVD (or your live talk) – *Session 1 Part 2: Building strong relationships* (32 minutes)

10:57   Small group discussion (see questions for ten-week courses in the guest manual)

11:30   End punctually. Encourage the guests to complete Exercise 2 of the homework before next time

Live talks: if appropriate, finish session with a short prayer. For example:

"Lord, we thank You that our children are a gift from You; thank You that they are each unique and have their own unique personality and gifts. Thank You for the privilege of parenting them, of shaping and influencing their lives. We ask You to help us with this challenging task. And we pray that, as a result of this course, each parent would feel more confident and better equipped for this role. We ask this in Jesus' name, Amen"

Week 3
Session 2 – Meeting our Teenagers' Needs, Part 1

10:00   Welcome guests and offer something to eat and drink

10:15   Review

"Look in your manual at a summary of what has been covered so far. Tell somebody else in your group what has been most relevant for you and if you organized any 'Family Time' over this past week. If so, talk about how it went"

10:25   Start the DVD (or your live talk) – *Session 2 Part 1: The five love languages* (33 minutes)

10:58   Ask guests to complete the exercise *Ranking the Love Languages* and then have a small group discussion (see questions for ten-week courses in the guest manual)

11:30   End punctually. Encourage the guests to complete Exercise 1 of the homework before next time

If appropriate, finish session with a short prayer.
For example:
*"Lord, we thank You for the assurance of Your love for us.
Thank You that You pour your love into our hearts by Your
Spirit. Please help us to show love to our teenagers in ways
that will assure them of our love and will give them the
confidence they need to be the people You have created
them to be. We ask this in Jesus' name, Amen"*

Week 4
Session 2 – Meeting our Teenagers' Needs, Part 2

10:00 Welcome guests and offer something to eat and drink

10:15 Review
*"Discuss with one or two others whether using one of the
love languages has made a difference in your family life
over this past week"*

10:25 Start the DVD (or your live talk) – *Session 2 Part 2:
Effective communication* (26 minutes)

10:51 *"Please complete the exercise in your manual,* Reflecting
Back. *In pairs one person pretends to be a teenager and
the other person pretends to be the parent. The 'teenager'
takes no more than a minute to tell the 'parent' something
he or she is upset or worried about. The parent listens and
then reflects back what they think the teenager is feeling.
Resist the desire to give advice or to reassure. The aim is to
practice empathizing with what the teenager is feeling but
may or may not be able to articulate. After continuing the
conversation for a minute or two, swap roles"*

11:05 Small group discussion (see questions for ten-week courses
in the guest manual)

11:30 End punctually. Encourage the guests to complete
Exercise 2 of the homework before next time

Live talks: if appropriate, finish session with a short prayer.
For example:
"Lord, we thank You that You are always listening to us and that we can pour out our hearts to You. Thank You for all the ways you assure us of Your love. We pray that You would help us to love our children with our time, words, touch, presents, and actions, and that you'd give us insight to know which love language is most significant for each child to feel loved. And in those families where communication between a parent and a teenager has broken down, we pray for a breakthrough and for a new start. We ask this in Jesus' name, Amen"

Week 5
Session 3 – Setting Boundaries, Part 1

10:00 Welcome guests and offer something to eat and drink

10:15 Review
       "Discuss whether using one of the five love languages or putting into practice any of the points on listening we looked at last week has made a difference in your relationship with a teenager"

10:25 Start the DVD (or your live talk) – *Session 3 Part 1: Letting go gradually* (30 minutes)

10:55 Exercise and discussion
       Ask guests to complete the exercise *Exercising Authority* and then have a small group discussion (see questions for ten-week courses in the guest manual)

11:30 End punctually. Encourage guests to complete Exercise 1 of the homework before next time
       If appropriate, finish session with a short prayer.
       For example:
       "Lord, we thank You that You have shown us the right ways to live and You guide us by your Spirit. We pray that You would give us wisdom as we seek to set boundaries for our children in the context of love. Help us to go at the right speed in giving them increasing freedom and responsibility. We ask this in Jesus' name, Amen"

Week 6
Session 3 – Setting Boundaries, Part 2

10:00 Welcome guests and offer something to eat and drink

10:15 Review
"Look back in your manual to remind yourself of what we covered last week and then discuss with one or two others what was most helpful for you"

10:25 Start the DVD (or your live talk) – *Session 3 Part 2: Encouraging responsibility* (27 minutes)

10:52 Small group discussion (see questions for ten-week courses in the guest manual)

11:30 End punctually. Encourage guests to complete Exercise 2 of the homework before next time

Live talks: if appropriate, finish session with a short prayer. For example:
"Lord, we thank You that You guide us and show us the best way to live. Thank You that you give us Your love and Your boundaries that we might live life to the full. Please help us to guide our teenagers so that they grow in trust and responsibility and become people who look out for others. Help us to give You our fears and our longings so that, as we let our children go, they may know a sense of freedom in becoming the people You've made them to be. We ask this in Jesus' name, Amen"

Week 7
Session 4 – Developing Emotional Health, Part 1

10:00 Welcome guests with something to eat and drink

10:15 Review

"Think of an example of a boundary you needed to impose with a child this week. What was the result?"

10:25 Start the DVD (or your live talk) – *Session 4 Part 1: Handling anger (ours and theirs)* (29 minutes)

10:54 Exercise and discussion

Ask guests to complete the exercise *Expressions of Anger* and then have a small group discussion (see questions for ten-week courses in the guest manual)

11:30 End punctually. Encourage guests to complete Exercise 1 of the homework before next time

If appropriate, finish with a short prayer.
For example:
"Lord, thank You that You have made us emotional beings, capable of feeling love and anger. We pray You would help us to set an example through controlling our anger and making our home a safe place for our children to express their emotions, both the positive and the negative, in constructive ways. We ask this in Jesus' name, Amen"

Week 8
Session 4 – Developing Emotional Health, Part 2

10:00 Welcome guests with something to eat and drink

10:15 Review

"Discuss what you realized about handling your own and your children's anger last week. What difference has it made?"

10:25 Start the DVD (or your live talk) – *Session 4 Part 2: Resolving conflict and handling stress* (31 minutes)

10:56 Small group discussion (see questions for ten-week courses in the guest manual)

11:30 End punctually. Encourage guests to complete Exercises 2 and 3 of the homework before next time

Live talks: if appropriate, finish session with a short prayer. For example:
"Lord, we thank You that You are the God of love and the Prince of peace. Thank You that You show us the way to resolve conflict and to build strong relationships in our family. We pray that You would help us to grow in our relationships with our children. May we learn to handle our anger and our stress in a healthy way, and equip our teenagers to do the same. And where a relationship between a parent and a teenager has become strained, please bring Your encouragement and hope for the future. Draw them closer again we pray. We ask this in Jesus' name. Amen"

Week 9
Session 5 – Helping Them Make Good Choices, Part 1

10:00 Welcome guests with something to eat and drink

10:15 Review

"Discuss whether any of the 'Six principles for resolving conflict' *have been helpful for you over the past week and whether you have put into practice any of the ways of helping teenagers to manage stress"*

10:25 Start the DVD (or your live talk) – *Session 5 Part 1: Giving a longer perspective* (35 minutes)

11:00 Small group discussion (see questions for ten-week courses in the guest manual)

11:30 End punctually. Encourage guests to complete Exercise 1 of the homework before next time

If appropriate, finish with a short prayer. For example:
"Lord, we thank You that You guard and protect us. We pray that You would use us to equip our children as they face temptation and big challenges. Help us to pass on to them the information and the values they need to make good choices. We ask this in Jesus' name, Amen"

Week 10
Session 5 – Helping Them Make Good Choices, Part 2

10:00 Welcome guests with something to eat and drink

10:15 Announcements (as applicable) and review

– *"Do please take advantage of the opportunity to buy some of the recommended books at the end of the session"*

– *"Please take as many invitations for the next Parenting Teenagers Course as you like to give to anyone you think would be interested in coming"*

– *"The Marriage Course is a very good follow-up to this course for anybody parenting as a couple. If that applies to you, please come on our next course and take invitations to give to others"*

– *"The Alpha course provides an opportunity to explore the meaning of life and to discuss the claims of the Christian faith. Doing Alpha has helped many parents to work out what beliefs and values they want to pass on to their children. Please take an invitation to our next course"*

– *"It would be helpful if you could take a few minutes to complete the feedback questionnaire. This acts as a review for you of the whole course and your comments will help us to run the course more effectively in the future. We will give you a few minutes to fill in your comments on this session before we finish"*

(A copy of the questionnaire can be downloaded from our website: **alphausa.org/relationshipcentral (in Canada– relationshipcentral.ca)**

10:30 Start the DVD (or your live talk) –
Session 5 Part 2: Equipping our children
(22 minutes)

10:52 Small group discussion (see questions for ten-week courses in the guest manual)

11.30 End punctually. Ask guests to complete the feedback questionnaire and hand it in before they leave

Live talks: if appropriate, finish session with a short prayer. For example:

"Lord, we thank You that love always protects, always trusts, always hopes, always perseveres, that love never fails. Thank You that You know and understand the challenges faced by each parent as they guide their teenagers to make good choices. We pray that You would help each of us to keep loving our children when things are difficult so that we might build, or rebuild, a close connection now and in the future. Lord, please fulfil Your purposes for each child and may their characters grow to reflect Your love and kindness. We ask this in Jesus' name, Amen"

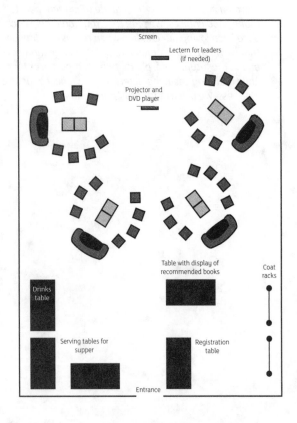

Screen

Lectern for leaders
(if needed)

Projector and
DVD player

Table with display of
recommended books

Coat
racks

Drinks
table

Serving tables for
supper

Registration
table

Entrance

Note: the tables used for the small groups can be two small tables
joined together (as indicated here) or one larger one.

Contact
information

Relationship Central c/o Alpha U.S.A.
2275 Half Day Road
Suite 185
Deerfield, IL 60015
Tel: 800.362.5742
Tel: + 212.406.5269
e-mail: info@alphausa.org
www.alphausa.org
www.alphausa.org/relationshipcentral

Alpha in the Caribbean
Holy Trinity Brompton
Brompton Road
London SW7 1JA UK
Tel: +44 (0) 845.644.7544
e-mail: americas@alpha.org
www.alpha.org

Relationship Central c/o Alpha Canada
Suite #230 – 11331 Coppersmith Way
Riverside Business Park
Richmond, BC V7A 5J9
Tel: 800.743.0899
Fax: 604.271.6124
e-mail: office@alphacanada.org
www.alphacanada.org
www.relationshipcentral.ca

To purchase resources in Canada:

David C. Cook Distribution Canada
P.O. Box 98, 55 Woodslee Avenue
Paris, ON N3L 3E5
Tel: 800.263.2664
Fax: 800.461.8575
e-mail: custserve@davidccook.ca
www.davidccook.ca

Also by Nicky and Sila Lee

'Provides real insight into how to be a good parent'
Bear Grylls

NICKY & SILA LEE
Best selling authors of **The Marriage Book**

THE
PARENTING
BOOK

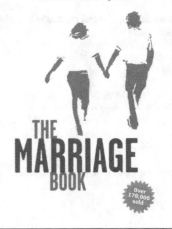

NICKY & SILA LEE
Authors of **The Parenting Book**

THE
MARRIAGE
BOOK

Over
170,000
sold